The Discovery Books are prepared

under the educational supervision of

Mary C. Austin, Ed.D.

Reading Specialist and

Professor of Education

Western Reserve University

A DISCOVERY BOOK

GARRARD PUBLISHING COMPANY
CHAMPAIGN, ILLINOIS

N
S

John F. Kennedy

New Frontiersman

by Charles P. Graves

illustrated by Paul Frame

For my son,

John P. Graves

Contents

John F. Kennedy:
New Frontiersman

Chapter *1*

"Old Ironsides"

Jack Kennedy paused on the gangplank of the *USS Constitution*. The old sailing ship was docked at the Navy Yard in Charlestown, Massachusetts.

He stared at the cannons peeping through the portholes of the gun deck. He tried to imagine the ship firing at an enemy vessel.

"Hurry up, Jack," his older brother, Joe, Jr., said, giving him a shove from behind. "We haven't got all day."

"Stop pushing me!" Jack turned and doubled up his fists.

"Boys, if you start fighting again I'll take you right home," Mrs. Kennedy warned. "We have plenty of time."

Mrs. Kennedy enjoyed taking her children to the historical sites near their home in Brookline, a suburb of Boston. She liked history and wanted her sons to like it too.

"How old is the *Constitution?*" Jack asked the guide who came to greet them.

"How old are you?" The guide smiled at the small, thin boy with the mop of unruly hair.

"Eight," Jack said. "I was born on May 29, 1917."

"Well, son, this ship is slightly older.

One hundred and twenty years older, to be exact. She was launched in this harbor in 1797.

"A few years later America got into a war with Tripoli, a nation in North Africa. The *Constitution* led America to victory. The peace treaty was signed on 'Old Ironsides.' "

"Why is the *Constitution* called 'Old Ironsides'? " Joe asked. "Her sides are made of wood, aren't they?"

"Yes," the guide said. "But it's mighty tough wood. During the War of 1812 the *Constitution* fought a battle with the *Guerriere,* a big English warship. A cannonball fired by the *Guerriere* hit the side of the *Constitution*. Instead of going through the wood it bounced into the water.

" 'You'd think the *Constitution's* sides were made of iron!' an American sailor said.

"The *Constitution* beat the English warship and captured her crew. Later she was nicknamed 'Old Ironsides.' "

Jack went over and patted one of the big black cannons. The guide told him how they were fired. He showed the boys cutlasses, boarding pikes, powder horns and flintlock guns.

Jack closed his eyes. He imagined himself boarding an enemy ship, waving a cutlass.

On their way home Mrs. Kennedy said, "When your Grandfather Fitzgerald was in Congress he helped save the *Constitution*. He found the ship rotting away at Portsmouth, New Hampshire.

In 1897, he asked Congress to put up enough money to restore the old ship.

"Now it has to be restored again. Children all over America are sending their pennies to save the ship. I know it would please your grandfather if you sent money too."

Besides serving in Congress, John F. Fitzgerald had been mayor of Boston. The boys' other grandfather, Patrick J. Kennedy, was active in politics too. Both men were Democrats. And both of their fathers had come from Ireland. They were proud of that.

They were proud of their grand-children too. Jack and Joe, Jr., had four sisters in 1925. Rosemary was six, Kathleen, five, Eunice, four, and Patricia was a baby.

When the boys reached home they told their sisters about their trip to the *Constitution*.

That night Jack stayed awake thinking about the old ship. He wondered if he would ever join the Navy.

Many years later, when Jack was President of the United States, he remembered his boyhood visit to "Old Ironsides."

He said that the sight of that historic old ship with its tall masts and black guns *"stirred my imagination and made American history come alive for me."*

Chapter *2*

School and Scouts

Jack's father, Joseph P. Kennedy, was a successful businessman. His business interests were then in New York City. He moved his family there in 1926.

The Kennedys lived in a big house in a part of the city called Riverdale. Jack went to Riverdale Country School, a short walk from home.

Later the Kennedys moved to Bronxville, a nearby suburb. Now Jack went to Riverdale School by bus.

One morning he was standing in front of his house when the bus drove up. His shoelaces were untied, his hair was uncombed, and his shirttail was hanging out. He was munching on toast.

Jack climbed on the bus, holding his books in one hand and his toast in the other. As the bus started up, Jack fell against a boy named Manuel Angulo.

"Get off!" Manuel cried, pushing Jack.

"Don't talk to me like that," Jack snapped. Jack and Manuel started fighting. Before either was hurt they were separated.

Jack knew he had a hot temper, but he was trying to learn to control it. After he calmed down he shook hands with Manuel. Jack and "Manolo," as Manuel was called, became good friends.

Both boys went out for the football team at school. They tried hard but seldom got to play in the games.

When Jack was twelve years old he and Manolo joined the Boy Scouts in Bronxville. They became members of the Raven Patrol of Troop 2.

Jack learned to recite the scout oath or promise. As long as he lived he never forgot the words, *"On my honor I will do my best to do my duty to God and my country . . ."*

Troop 2 went on a camping trip to Bear Mountain. Jack enjoyed hiking, sending messages with signal flags and learning about nature.

Now that he was a scout he thought he should have a bigger allowance. Jack wrote a letter to his father.

"My recent allowance is 40c. This I used for . . . playthings of childhood but now I am a scout and I put away my childish things. . . . I have to buy canteens, haversacks, blankets, searchlichgs poncho things that will last for years . . . and so I put in my plea for a raise of thirty cents for me to buy scout things . . ."

Jack wrote "searchlichgs" for searchlights. He was not a good speller. But he read a great deal. He liked history and made good grades in it.

One of his teachers at Riverdale, Mrs. Guiney, says that he was a *"capable student. Jack was a good boy. If he wasn't I could tell you much more."*

Chapter *3*

"Most Likely to Succeed"

When Jack was thirteen he left home for the first time. He went to the Canterbury School in New Milford, Connecticut.

At first, Jack was homesick. But he soon got over it.

He tried to make the football team, but he wasn't big enough. Then he went out for swimming. He worked hard and was able to swim the 50-yard dash in 30 seconds.

He wrote home, *"We are reading Ivanhoe in English and although I may not be able to remember material things such as tickets, gloves, and so on, I can remember things like Ivanhoe, and the last time we had an exam on it I got ninety-eight."*

During Easter vacation Jack had an attack of appendicitis. He could not go back to Canterbury.

The next fall he entered Choate, a boarding school for boys, in Wallingford, Connecticut. His brother Joe was also at Choate, two classes ahead of Jack.

Jack went out for sports. He played football, basketball, golf and tennis. His marks were good, but not as good as they could have been. He didn't study hard enough.

"*Now Jack,*" his father wrote, "*I don't want to give the impression that I am a nagger, for goodness knows, that is the worst thing a parent can be. After long experience in sizing up people I definitely know you have the goods and you can go a long way. Now aren't you foolish not to get all there is out of what God has given you . . . I am urging you to do the best you can.*"

Jack loved his father and wanted to please him. But he found some subjects hard to master. He made good grades in history and English because they were his favorite subjects.

When school ended the Kennedys went to Hyannis Port on Cape Cod. They had a house by the sea. The children swam, played tennis and sailed.

They also played touch football. Each Kennedy played hard, even the girls.

Joe and Jack competed with each other in many sports. But sometimes they teamed up for sailing races. They always tried to win. The stronger the competition, the better they liked it.

"When the going gets tough," their father often said, *"the tough get going."*

Mr. Kennedy bought a boat that was large enough for his whole family. There were now two more children, Bobby and Jean. This meant there were ten Kennedys in all. They named the boat the *Tenofus*. When Teddy was born, Mr. Kennedy bought another boat. It was named *Onemore* in honor of Teddy.

Each fall the older boys went to Choate. Jack had many friends there.

His roommate, LeMoyne Billings, was an easygoing boy who was full of fun.

When Jack was a senior his father promised him a trip to Europe if he made better grades.

"Let's stop fooling around," Jack said to LeMoyne, "we're not working hard enough."

Jack and his roommate began paying more attention to their studies. Jack was also busy working on *The Brief,* the Choate yearbook. He was the business manager.

He sold a great deal of advertising for *The Brief* and made it a financial success. Perhaps that was one reason why his classmates voted him the *"most likely to succeed."*

LeMoyne was voted the *"best natured."*

Chapter 4

"A Swell Guy"

In fall, 1936, Jack entered Harvard College in Cambridge, Massachusetts. His father had gone to Harvard and Joe, Jr., was already there. Joe was making good grades, and he played on the football team. Everybody liked him.

Jack still liked sports, and he went out for several teams. He made friends with Torbert H. Macdonald, who was one of Harvard's best football players. Jack and "Torby," as he was called, became roommates.

Jack didn't make the first team, but he played on the junior varsity. He tried so hard that he hurt his back.

Jack's back bothered him for the rest of his life. But he was able to keep on with sports. His best sport was swimming. He swam the backstroke in many meets. The one he wanted to swim in most was with Yale.

Shortly before the meet he got a cold. He had to go to the college hospital.

Jack was worried because he was missing swimming practice. Torby helped him sneak out of the hospital when nobody was looking. He went to the pool and practiced. Then he slipped back into the hospital.

Finally the doctors let him out. The team was having tryouts for the meet.

The fastest men would be picked to swim against Yale.

Jack tried out for the backstroke. He was still weak from his illness. He did his best, but another Harvard swimmer beat him. Jack didn't get to swim against Yale.

During his first two years at Harvard, Jack's grades were nothing to brag about. He seemed more interested in sports than in studying.

Jack was a tall young man with a friendly smile. But he wasn't very neat. Once he was dressing to go out. He dropped his old clothes on the floor.

"Watch the way you're throwing things around, Jack," Torby said. "Our room is beginning to look like a rummage sale."

"Don't be so sanctimonious," Jack cried. "Whose stuff do you think I'm throwing mine on top of? Yours!"

Late in 1937, Jack's father was made Ambassador to England. His job was to look after the interests of the United States in London. All the Kennedys moved to England except Joe and Jack.

The next summer they went over, too, and had a happy reunion. Bobby was now twelve years old. He was glad to see his older brothers.

Jack became interested in European politics. His father's job made him feel close to public affairs.

That fall at Harvard Jack began to work harder. He was studying history, government and politics. He tried to keep up with current events.

Many people felt there would be a big war in Europe soon. Adolph Hitler ruled Germany and Benito Mussolini ruled Italy. These dictators had strong armies. They wanted to take land from other countries.

Jack wanted to learn about this war firsthand. Harvard let him spend part of his junior year in Europe.

He was in London in September, 1939, when the Germans invaded Poland. England was not prepared for war, but she had promised to help Poland. So England declared war on Germany. France followed England, and World War II began.

Jack returned to Harvard for his senior year. He worked harder than he ever had before.

Now he wanted to make good grades as much as he had wanted to swim against Yale.

He wrote his final paper on the reasons why England was unprepared for war. It was so good that it was later published as a book called *Why England Slept.*

In June, he was graduated from Harvard *cum laude* in political science. *Cum laude* means "with praise." His final paper got *magna cum laude.* That means "with great praise."

Jack got a cablegram from London. It read, *"Two things I always knew about you. One that you are smart. Two that you are a swell guy. Love, Dad."*

Chapter *5*

War in the Pacific

Jack joined the Navy in 1941. A few months later the Japanese bombed American ships in Hawaii. Now the United States was in World War II on the side of England, France and Russia.

Joe, Jr., joined the Navy too. He was a flyer and was sent to Europe.

Jack went to the South Pacific. He was put in command of a fast patrol torpedo boat, the PT-109. It was a small boat with a crew of thirteen.

Shortly after midnight on August 2, 1943, Kennedy's boat was patrolling the waters around the Solomon Islands. It was looking for enemy ships to sink.

Lieutenant Kennedy was at the wheel. All the men on the boat were peering into the darkness. Suddenly, someone shouted, "Ship off the starboard bow!"

A big Japanese destroyer was racing toward the tiny PT-109.

"Full speed ahead!" Jack signaled. It was too late. The enemy destroyer struck the PT-109, cut it in half, and plowed on into the night.

Kennedy was hurled against the side of the boat. His back was hurt again. But he had no time to think about it.

Lieutenant Kennedy and most of his men were up in the bow of the boat.

It was afloat, but Kennedy ordered the men into the sea. The gas tanks were leaking. He feared they might explode.

Some of the men were already in the water. And two had been killed when the destroyer struck.

The gasoline spread over the sea and caught fire. The men tried to fan the flames away. When the fire was out, Kennedy and some of the men swam back to the boat.

"McMahon is badly burned," called Charles Harris, a gunner's mate. "Can you help him, skipper?" Patrick Mc-Mahon was the oldest man in the crew.

Kennedy dived into the sea and towed McMahon back to the boat.

Then Harris was in trouble. His leg was injured. Kennedy went to help.

"Skipper," Harris said, "I can't swim any more."

"Try," Kennedy said.

"I'll never make it."

Kennedy yelled into his ear. *"For a guy from Boston you're really putting on some exhibition out here, Harris."*

Harris had a lot of courage. He tried, and with Kennedy's help he reached the boat.

But the boat was slowly sinking, and there were no lifeboats. Soon they would have to swim.

The sun rose like a ball of fire. Kennedy pointed to a group of islands three and a half miles away. "We'll swim to one of those islands. The Japs are probably on the bigger ones. Plum Pudding Island should be safe."

McMahon was too badly burned to swim. Kennedy held the straps of McMahon's life jacket in his teeth. He started towing him through the water.

The rest of the men followed in their life jackets. They knew there were sharks in the water. And they knew enemy planes might shoot at them at any minute. But they pushed doggedly ahead, holding a plank.

After four hours the men staggered ashore. The island was deserted. They crawled up the beach and flopped down to rest.

Kennedy decided to try to get help. He knew that other PT boats often patrolled Ferguson Passage, a waterway between the islands. When it was dark Kennedy swam out into the passage.

He floated in the water a long time. But no PT boats appeared.

Kennedy swam back toward Plum Pudding. There was a strong current. He was swept up on another deserted island. He fell asleep at once. When he woke up he swam back to his men.

Every day Kennedy tried a new way to get help. He moved the exhausted men to another island nearer Ferguson Passage. Still no PT boats appeared.

The men were almost starving now. They had nothing but coconuts to eat.

Six days went by. Kennedy and another officer, named Ross, swam to one island after another. Finally they returned with treasure, candy they had found in a crate washed up on a beach. The crew had an even greater treasure.

Two natives in a canoe had come ashore and offered to help.

Kennedy scratched a message on a coconut with a knife. He asked the natives to take it to an island occupied by friendly forces.

An Australian Navy officer got the message. He sent a rescue party. At last Kennedy and his men were safe.

Kennedy was awarded the Navy and Marine Corps Medal for his part in saving his crew.

The citation read:

"His courage, endurance and excellent leadership contributed to the saving of several lives and was in keeping with the highest traditions of the United States Naval Service . . ."

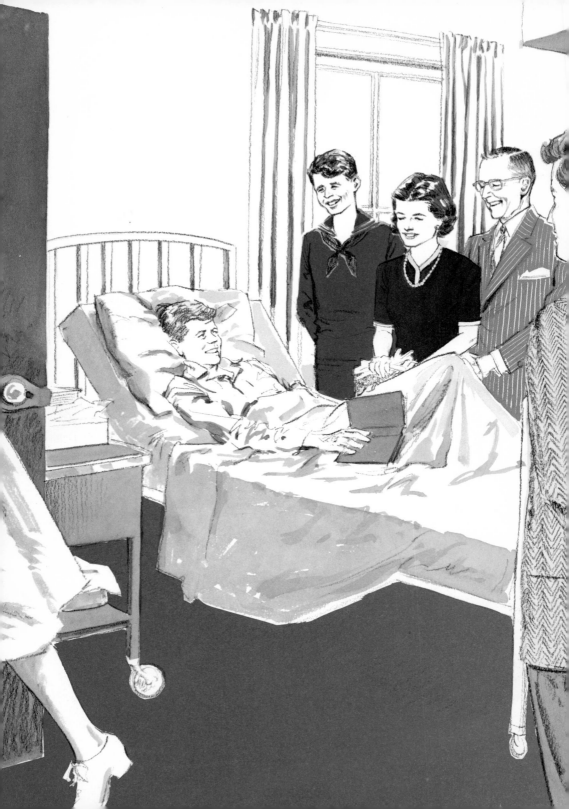

Chapter *6*

Politics

Kennedy's back had been seriously hurt when his boat was hit by the destroyer. He was sent to the United States. His back was operated on in Massachusetts early in 1944.

Kennedy read about the battles the allied armies were winning in Europe. He knew the war would end soon. He looked forward to seeing Joe again.

But in August he heard terrible news. Joe's plane had exploded in the air while he was on a secret mission. Joe was killed.

Jack and all his family were heartbroken. Jack got the Kennedys and Joe's friends to write a book. The book was named *As We Remember Joe.*

Jack wrote ". . . *there is a completeness to Joe's life, and that is the completeness of perfection. His life as he lived, and finally died, could hardly have been improved upon.*"

Many more young Americans were being killed. But at last, in 1945, the war ended. The United States and her allies had won.

Jack was no longer in the Navy. He had to decide what he wanted to do.

His father was a very rich man. He had given his children enough money so that they would not have to earn any. He wanted them to help other people.

Jack decided to run for Congress from the 11th Massachusetts District. He was a Democrat so he entered the Democratic primary.

There were nine other people in the race. Jack worked harder than any of them. In his first speech he said he had made a promise during the war.

"When ships were sinking and young Americans were dying . . . I firmly resolved to serve my country in peace as I honestly tried to serve it in war."

Jack was tousle-haired and skinny. He looked almost like a boy. But the people in the 11th District liked him.

They were from many parts of the world. Jack drank tea with the Chinese and coffee with the Syrians. He ate corned beef and cabbage with the Irish and spaghetti with the Italians. He made more than 400 speeches.

Some of his opponents made fun of him. One called him the *"poor little rich kid."*

Kennedy usually paid no attention to such words. He talked about what he would do if elected. He promised to try to get the people better houses, lower rents and better jobs.

On primary election day Kennedy went to the polls with his Grandmother and Grandfather Fitzgerald. Later, they learned the news. Jack had won by thousands of votes.

Grandfather Fitzgerald was so happy that he danced an Irish jig and sang *Sweet Adeline*.

Kennedy beat his Republican opponent in the November election. He took his seat in Congress early in 1947. He was 29 years old, but looked much younger. There were many jokes about his being mistaken for a page boy.

He was still not very neat. Sometimes he came to the Capitol with his shirt-tail hanging out.

But Kennedy kept his eyes and ears open. He was learning a great deal about politics and how the government was run.

He was happy in Washington. He played touch football and went sailing on the Potomac River.

Soon, however, there was another tragedy in his life. His gay young sister, Kathleen, whom he called Kick, was killed in a plane accident.

In the book about Joe, Kick had written: *"I know the one thing Joe would never want is that we should feel sad and gloomy about life without him. Instead, he'd laugh with that wonderful twinkle shining out of his Irish eyes and say, 'Gee, can't you all learn to get along without me?'"*

Now Jack would have to learn to get along without Kick too.

Chapter 7

Pulitzer Prize

Kennedy decided to run for Senator from Massachusetts in 1952. His family pitched in to help.

Mrs. Kennedy gave a series of tea parties. "New-type Boston Tea Parties" they were called. Thousands of women came to the parties to meet her son.

Bobby, Teddy and the Kennedy girls worked hard for their brother too.

It was a close election, but John Fitzgerald Kennedy won. In January, 1953, he took his seat in the Senate.

Senator Kennedy was now 36 years old. He had been so busy that he had never married. Many people called him the most eligible bachelor in America.

The year before he had met a beautiful girl named Jacqueline Lee Bouvier at a dinner party. Later he said, *"I leaned across the asparagus and asked for a date."*

Now Kennedy saw "Jackie" more and more. He took her to dinner and the movies.

Soon they were married. Jackie tried hard to be a regular Kennedy. She entered all their sports. She even broke an ankle playing touch football.

But Kennedy couldn't play football as hard as he once did. The operation in 1944 had not been a complete success. His back was again bothering him a great deal.

Finally he went to the hospital. His back was operated on two times. His doctors told him to take a long rest. He went to Palm Beach, Florida, where his parents had a house.

Kennedy kept busy even while resting. He had always been interested in courage, both physical and political. He wrote a book about politicians who had showed courage. These men had always done what they thought was right, even though it hurt their careers.

The book was named *Profiles in Courage*. He dedicated it to Jackie.

"It is a splendid flag that Senator Kennedy has nailed to his mast," a newspaper writer said about the book.

Profiles in Courage helped make Kennedy well known all over America. He was almost nominated for vice-president in 1956.

The following year his book won the Pulitzer Prize for biography. Kennedy was proud that it was so successful. But he was even prouder about what happened on November 27, 1957. His first child, Caroline, was born.

Chapter *8*

President

In 1958, Kennedy ran again for the Senate. He won by 874,608 votes. It was the greatest political victory in the history of Massachusetts.

The election proved that Kennedy was very popular with the voters. People all over the United States began to think that Kennedy should run for President in 1960.

During the next two years he made many speeches throughout the country. People flocked to hear him and shake his hand.

Kennedy was a Roman Catholic. No Catholic had ever been President. Some non-Catholics thought Kennedy might not believe in separation of church and state. This is one of the ideas on which America was founded.

Kennedy put these fears to rest. He said that he believed in the separation of church and state.

Bobby Kennedy was his brother's campaign manager. He helped Jack get the Democratic nomination for President. All the other Kennedys helped, as usual, during the campaign.

Richard M. Nixon was the Republican candidate. Millions of Americans voted. The election was extremely close, but Kennedy won.

He was the youngest man and the first Catholic ever elected President.

Soon after the election the Kennedys' second child—a boy—was born. He was named John Fitzgerald Kennedy, Jr. His birthday came just two days before Caroline's.

Kennedy was sworn in as the 35th President of the United States on January 20, 1961. Thousands of his friends came to Washington to watch. Among them were members of the crew of PT-109.

Kennedy made one of the finest inaugural speeches in American history.

He told the world that the United States has always stood for freedom, and that she would pay any price to keep that freedom.

He promised the people in poorer countries that the United States would help them help themselves. He asked all Americans to join him in the fight against the evils of *"poverty, disease and war itself . . .*

"And so, my fellow Americans," he ended, *"ask not what your country can do for you—ask what you can do for your country . . . let us go forth to lead the land we love . . . knowing that here on earth God's work must truly be our own."*

Chapter *9*

In the White House

Kennedy carried his love of American history into the White House. There was a model of "Old Ironsides" on his office mantelpiece. Pictures of the ship's fight with the *Guerriere* hung on the walls.

Jackie liked American history too. She gathered the finest art and furniture America had produced. She put them in the White House where all the people could see them.

The Kennedys made the White House the center of American culture. They invited scientists, poets, artists, writers, musicians, actors and athletes to visit them.

It had been many years since little children had lived in the President's mansion. Now the rooms rang with the shouts of Caroline and her friends. They raced their tricycles down the halls. The children had a school on the third floor. The President visited it often. There was a playground on the White House lawn.

Caroline had several pets. Among them were a dog named Charlie, a cat named Tom Kitten and two hamsters, named Debbie and Billie. Once the hamsters escaped and hid under the President's bed.

Kennedy was the busiest man in the nation. But he always found time for his children. One of Caroline's favorite books was *The Three Bears*.

"Read me," she would say, climbing into her father's lap.

The Kennedys spent many weekends in Virginia. There Caroline rode her pony, Macaroni. Mrs. Kennedy had won ribbons at horse shows as a girl. She taught Caroline to be a good rider.

John F. Kennedy, Jr., was just a baby when his father became President. The President called him John-John. Caroline said he was her "kissing baby."

When John-John was older he liked to visit his father's office. He hid under the desk and played bunny rabbit while his father worked.

In the summer the President had fun with his nephews and nieces in Hyannis Port. To them he was just Uncle Jack. He piled them in his golf cart and took them to a store for candy.

Children everywhere liked their new President. Many sent him letters. He answered all he could.

One boy wrote that he would like to live in the White House. *"Sorry,"* the President replied, *"you will have to wait your turn."*

One day the President read about a boy who had been a hero on his school bus. The bus driver had a heart attack and fell off his seat while the bus was moving. Ten-year-old Steven Eicker jumped behind the wheel and slammed on the brakes. He stopped the bus.

The President wrote to Steve. *"You showed great courage . . . You saved many of your schoolmates from harm. We are very proud of you, Steven."*

Kennedy was the first Boy Scout ever to be elected President of the United States. One day a scout named Bill Fair gave him a "mile-swim" card. It was back-dated to August 2, 1943, the day Kennedy swam ashore from his wrecked PT boat.

Kennedy read the card aloud. *"This is to certify that John Fitzgerald Kennedy swam a full mile under safe conditions."*

The President and his office workers roared with laughter. They knew that his swim through the dangerous waters had been anything but safe.

However, the President did not laugh all the time. He worried about many problems, including war. He knew that if nuclear war came millions of people would be killed.

"It really does not matter as far as you and I are concerned," he once said to a friend. *"What really matters is all the children."*

Chapter *10*

The New Frontier

"I call upon all of you," Kennedy told the nation, *"to join us in a journey to the new frontier."*

The new frontier was not a place but a way of life. Kennedy tried to make America push ahead in education, science, employment and other fields.

Kennedy often worked sixteen hours a day. He read four newspapers while he ate breakfast. He did "homework" at night, and read reports from his advisers. He wanted his government to be as good as possible.

Kennedy formed the Peace Corps. Peace Corps members taught the natives in underdeveloped countries to be better farmers and workers. Many young men and women joined the Peace Corps and worked abroad. They won respect for America throughout the world.

Sargent Shriver, President Kennedy's brother-in-law, was in charge of the Peace Corps. Other members of the President's family were in Washington too. Bobby Kennedy was appointed the Attorney General of the United States.

His job was to enforce the laws. Later the President's youngest brother, Teddy, was elected Senator from Massachusetts.

Early in 1962, an American astronaut was put in orbit around the earth. He was Lieutenant-Colonel John H. Glenn of the Marines.

Kennedy telephoned Glenn when he returned to earth. *"Colonel, we are really proud of you. And I must say you did a wonderful job."*

Kennedy was glad that the United States was catching up with Russia in space. He had asked Congress to give more money for space projects.

The next fall Kennedy had trouble with Russia close to home. He learned that the Russians were building missile bases in Cuba, 90 miles from Florida.

Nuclear missiles sent from Cuba could kill millions of Americans.

Kennedy did not want a war with Russia. But he was willing to risk war to have the missiles removed. He told the Navy to search ships going to Cuba. None with supplies for missile bases would be allowed to continue.

The whole world held its breath. Many people thought war was certain.

But Russia did not want war either. She agreed to remove the missile bases.

This was a great victory for Kennedy and the United States. Americans were proud of their courageous President.

Kennedy had problems at home too. The Supreme Court had said that white and Negro children should go to school together. This was a law of the land.

Some people did not want to obey this law. There were riots in parts of the country. Many people were hurt.

Kennedy went on television and asked Americans to end racial hatred. *"This nation was founded by men of many nations and backgrounds,"* he said. *"It was founded on the principle that all men are created equal . . ."* He told the people that Americans of any color should be able to enjoy life in America.

The President sent a Civil Rights bill to Congress. These laws that give Negroes the same rights as white people were passed a year later.

Being President was not an easy job. To relax, Kennedy took Caroline and John-John swimming in the big White House pool.

"Look what I can do!" each would cry. Kennedy would smile and forget his problems for a moment.

Most of all he worried about the possibility of nuclear war. For years both Russia and the United States had been testing nuclear weapons. These tests put radioactive material in the air in dangerous amounts. Kennedy wanted to stop the tests.

On July 25, 1963, a treaty was made between the United States, Russia and England. The nations agreed not to test nuclear weapons in space, in the air, or under water.

This was a great achievement of Kennedy's New Frontier.

Chapter *11*

The President Is Shot

President Kennedy woke up early the morning of November 22, 1963. He and Mrs. Kennedy were in Texas on a political trip. They had been having a fine time.

Caroline and John-John stayed in Washington. Kennedy hoped to return home in time for their birthdays.

The President left his Fort Worth hotel to greet a large crowd waiting outside. He apologized because Mrs. Kennedy was still dressing.

"Mrs. Kennedy is busy organizing herself," he said with a grin. *"It takes a little longer, you know. But then she looks so much better than we do."*

Later that morning the Kennedys flew to Dallas. The President was to speak there. Vice-President and Mrs. Lyndon Johnson were with the Kennedys. So were Governor and Mrs. John Connally of Texas. A big crowd met them at the Dallas airport. Kennedy shook hands with as many people as he could.

The Kennedys and the Connallys got in one car and the Johnsons in another. It was sunny; the tops of the cars were down. They started through Dallas.

Not all Texans liked Kennedy's ideas. But cheering people lined the streets. Kennedy was enjoying himself.

Mrs. Connally turned to him. *"You can't say that Dallas isn't friendly to you today."*

At that moment a shot rang out. The President slumped forward with a bullet hole in his neck. Another bullet hit his head.

"Oh, they have shot my husband!" Mrs. Kennedy cried. *"I love you, Jack."*

The car roared off to the nearest hospital. But nothing could be done for the President. He was dead.

An hour later Lyndon B. Johnson was sworn in as the 36th President of the United States.

The American people were heartbroken over Kennedy's tragic death. He had done so much for the land he loved. But he wanted to do so much more.

When his brother was killed Kennedy had written, *"His life as he lived . . . could hardly have been improved upon."* Now these words applied to John Fitzgerald Kennedy.

Kennedy never made his speech in Dallas. But he had written it before he died. His words live on.

"We in this country . . . are . . . the watchmen on the walls of world freedom. We ask . . . that we may achieve for our time and for all time the ancient vision of peace on earth, good will toward men."